DEPARTMENT OF THE AIR FORCE

PRESENTATION TO THE COMMITTEE ON ARMED SERVICES
UNITED STATES SENATE

FISCAL YEAR 2015 AIR FORCE POSTURE STATEMENT

STATEMENT OF: THE HONORABLE DEBORAH LEE JAMES
                  SECRETARY OF THE AIR FORCE

                  GENERAL MARK A. WELSH III
                  CHIEF OF STAFF, UNITED STATES AIR FORCE

APRIL 10, 2014

NOT FOR PUBLICATION UNTIL RELEASED
BY THE COMMITTEE ON ARMED SERVICES
UNITED STATES SENATE

TABLE OF CONTENTS

Introduction 1

Strategic Environment 1

Fiscal Environment 2

    Historical Perspective 2

    Fiscal Realities 2

    Effects of FY13 Budget and Sequestration 2

    FY14 Game Plan 3

    FY15 and Beyond - Long Range Vision 3

FY15 Budget Decision Methodology 4

    Full-Spectrum Readiness 4

    Fleet Divestment 5

    Active Component/Reserve Component (AC/RC) Mix 6

    Recapitalization vs. Modernization 7

Making Every Dollar Count 8

    Program Stewardship 8

    Energy 9

    Base Realignment and Closure (BRAC) 9

    Military Compensation 10

Airmen 10

    Innovative Force 10

    Airmen and Family Support 10

    Air Force Sexual Assault Prevention and Response 11

    Diversity 11

    Force Management 12

America's Air Force 12

    A Global, Ready Force 12

    Air Force Core Missions 12

Conclusion 16

INTRODUCTION

America's Airmen and Air Force capabilities play a foundational role in how our military fights and wins wars. The Air Force's agile response to national missions – in the time, place, and means of our choosing – gives our Nation an indispensable and unique advantage that we must retain as we plan for an uncertain future. Whether responding to a national security threat or a humanitarian crisis, your Air Force provides the responsive global capabilities necessary for the joint force to operate successfully.

It takes the combined efforts of all of our military Services and the whole of government to deny, deter, and defeat an enemy, and over the last decade this integration has tightened. Just as we depend on our joint partners, every other Service depends on the Air Force to do its job. Whether it is Global Positioning System (GPS) information to navigate waterways, airlift to get troops to and from the fight, manning intercontinental ballistic missile (ICBM) silos to deter aggression, or reconnaissance and satellite communication to tell forces where enemy combatants gather or hide, the Air Force provides these capabilities, as well as many others. Here at home, our Airmen patrol the skies ready to protect the homeland and are integral to the movement of people and lifesaving supplies when disasters, like Hurricane Sandy or the California wildfires, strike. This capability to see what is happening and project power anywhere in the world at any time is what *Global Vigilance, Global Reach,* and *Global Power* are all about.

The current fiscal environment requires the Air Force to make some very tough choices. When making decisions about the best way for the Air Force to support our Nation's defense, the abrupt and arbitrary nature of sequestration created a dilemma between having a ready force today or a modern force tomorrow. To best support national defense requirements, comply with the Defense Department's fiscal guidance, and meet defense strategy priorities, as updated by the 2014 Quadrennial Defense Review (QDR), we attempted to preserve capabilities to protect the homeland, build security globally, and project power and win decisively. To do this the Air Force emphasized capability over capacity. We worked hard to make every dollar count so we could protect the minimum capabilities for today's warfighting efforts, while also investing in capabilities needed to defeat potential high-end threats of the future. Moving forward, we seek to maintain a force ready for the full range of military operations while building an Air Force capable of executing our five core missions: 1) air and space superiority; 2) intelligence, surveillance, and reconnaissance (ISR); 3) rapid global mobility; 4) global strike; and 5) command and control, all against a well-armed and well-trained adversary in 2023 and beyond.

STRATEGIC ENVIRONMENT

The United States Air Force has long enjoyed technological superiority over any potential adversary. However, the spread of advanced technology has eroded this advantage faster than anticipated. The proliferation of nuclear weapons, cyber capabilities, cruise missiles, ballistic missiles, remotely piloted vehicles, air defense systems, anti-satellite development efforts, and technologically advanced aircraft, including 5th generation fighters, are particularly concerning. Increased access to such capabilities heightens the potential for the emergence of additional near-peer competitors—adversaries capable of producing, acquiring, and integrating high-end capabilities that rival or equal our own and can possibly deny our freedom of action. This means we may not be able to go where we need to in order to protect our national security interests. This dynamic security environment creates both opportunities and challenges for the United States. As we address known threats, we must also have the vision to understand the changing strategic landscape, and keep an open mind with regard to which of these changes represent true threats, and which may present strategic opportunities.

FISCAL ENVIRONMENT

HISTORICAL PERSPECTIVE

The Air Force has always had to balance what we can do (capability), how much we have to do it with (capacity), and how well trained and responsive we need to be (readiness). However, over time our trade space has been shrinking. As an Air Force, with respect to aircraft and personnel, we are on course to be the smallest since our inception in 1947. After peaking at 983,000 active component Airmen in 1952, we have consistently gotten smaller. While the military as a whole has grown since 9/11, the Air Force has further reduced our active component end strength from 354,000 to just over 327,600 today. Also, the Air Force post-war budget drawdowns in the 1950s and 1970s were followed by major acquisition programs that fielded most of our current missile, bomber, tanker, fighter, and cargo inventory, yet post 9/11 investments have replaced less than five percent of the currently active combat aircraft. Since 1990, our aircraft inventory has decreased from 9,000 to 5,400 aircraft, and the average aircraft age has increased from 17 to 27 years. Additionally, since 1962, our annual budget's non-Blue Total Obligation Authority (TOA) (funding that the Air Force does not control and cannot use to balance other requirements) has risen to more than 20 percent of our total Air Force TOA.

This narrow trade space and constrained funding leave no room for error. Past drawdown strategies suggest that the Air Force should prioritize high-end combat capabilities; near-term procurement of highly capable and cost-effective weapons and munitions as force multipliers; and long-term research and development for the next-generation weapon delivery platforms. Simultaneously, we must gain and maintain readiness across the full range of operations.

FISCAL REALITIES

In fiscal year 2015 (FY15), the Air Force must be able to execute national defense requirements while also recovering from the impacts of FY13 sequestration, and adjusting to the FY14 Bipartisan Budget Act (BBA) funding levels and the uncertainty in the future years planned budget top line for FY16 and beyond. We are working hard to make the right choices that maximize each taxpayer dollar and ensure we can meet national security needs today and in the future.

EFFECTS OF FY13 BUDGET AND SEQUESTRATION

The magnitude of the cuts generated in FY13 by sequestration was difficult to absorb in the short term. We stood down 31 active component squadrons for more than three months. We initiated civilian furloughs, putting extreme stress on the workload and personal finances of our civilian workforce. We cut maintenance of our facilities, in many cases by 50 percent, and delayed major maintenance actions, including depot aircraft overhauls.

With support from Congress, the Air Force was able to realign $1.7 billion into operations accounts. This allowed us to cover our overseas contingency operations requirements and enabled us to resume flying operations, but these budget adjustments came at a sacrifice to future weapon system modernization. Of the units affected by the FY13 sequestration, only about 50 percent have returned to their already degraded pre-sequestration combat ready proficiency levels, and it will take years to recover from the weapon system sustainment backlog.

FY14 GAME PLAN

Though the BBA and the FY14 Appropriations Act provided partial sequestration relief in FY14, and some help for FY15, they do not solve all of our problems. The additional funds help us reverse our immediate near-term readiness shortfalls and enable the Air Force to build a plan that mostly shields our highest priorities, including: flying hours; weapon system sustainment; top three investment programs; and key readiness requirements such as radars, ranges, and airfields. However, the tightening fiscal caps combined with the abrupt and arbitrary nature of sequestration clearly drove the Air Force into a "ready force today" versus a "modern force tomorrow" dilemma, forcing us to sacrifice future modernization for current readiness.

This dilemma is dangerous and avoidable and will continue to be a threat in 2015 and beyond. If given the flexibility to make prudent cuts over time and avoid sequestration, we can achieve significant savings and still maintain our ability to provide *Global Vigilance, Global Reach*, and *Global Power* for the Nation.

FY15 AND BEYOND - LONG RANGE VISION

The FY15 President's Budget (PB) is our effort to develop and retain the capabilities our Nation expects of its Air Force within the constraints placed upon us. The least disruptive and least risky way to manage a post-war drawdown is to wait until the end of the conflict to reduce spending and to provide a ramp to the cuts. Sequestration provides no such ramp. However, the FY15 PB in conjunction with the BBA does allow for a more manageable ramp, as seen in Chart I, *Air Force Budget Projections*. This funding profile allows us to move toward balance between capability, capacity, and readiness.

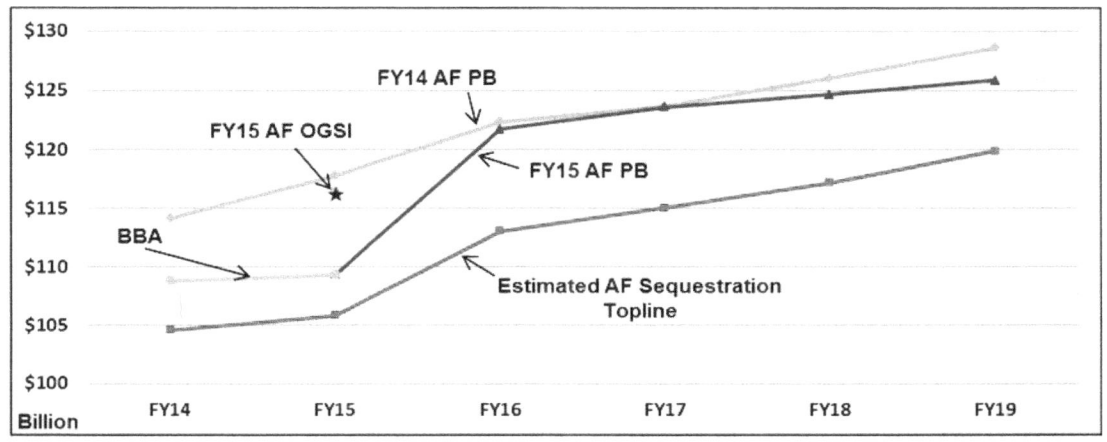

Chart I: Air Force Budget Projections

Maintaining the FY15 PB top line level of funding will provide the time and flexibility to make strategic resourcing choices to maximize combat capability from each taxpayer dollar. If we continue to be funded at the FY15 PB top line level we can continue a gradual path of recovery to full-spectrum combat readiness, preserve munitions inventories, and protect investments such as the new training aircraft system and the next generation of space-based systems. Additionally, the President has proposed an additional Opportunity, Growth, and Security Initiative (OGSI) to accompany the FY15 Budget Request. For the Air Force, this $7 billion additional investment would enhance our readiness posture, enable us to fund critical modernization programs, accelerate recapitalization efforts, and improve our installations and bases.

A sequestration-level budget would result in a very different Air Force. We are aggressively seeking innovative cost savings and more efficient and effective ways of accomplishing our missions, however these initiatives will not be sufficient to reach sequestration funding levels. To pay the sequestration-level bill we will have to sacrifice current tanker and ISR capacity by divesting KC-10 and RQ-4 Block 40 fleets, all of our major investment programs will be at risk, and our readiness recovery will be significantly slowed due to required cuts in weapon system sustainment and ranges.

FY15 BUDGET DECISION METHODOLOGY

During the development of the FY15 budget submission, the Air Force took a bold but realistic approach to support the Air Force 2023 framework and the 2012 Defense Strategic Guidance, as updated during deliberations on the 2014 QDR. To do this within fiscal guidance, including the Strategic Choices and Management Review, we had to make difficult trades between force structure (capacity), readiness, and modernization (capability). As a result, the Air Force established four guiding principles to steer our strategy and budget process.

> (1) We must remain ready for the full-spectrum of military operations;
> (2) When forced to cut capabilities (tooth), we must also cut the associated support structure and overhead (tail);
> (3) We will maximize the contribution of the Total Force; and
> (4) Our approach will focus on the unique capabilities the Air Force provides the joint force, especially against a full-spectrum, high-end threat.

When building the budget, there were no easy choices. We divested fleets and cut manpower that we would have preferred to retain. We focused on global, long-range, and multi-role capabilities, especially those that can operate in contested environments, which meant keeping key recapitalization programs on track. We made these choices because losing a future fight to a high-end adversary would be catastrophic.

FULL-SPECTRUM READINESS

Because of our global reach, speed of response, and lethal precision, the Air Force is the force that the Nation relies on to be first in for the high-end fight. This is our highest priority. To do this we must be ready across the entire force. This means we need to have the right number of Airmen, with the right equipment, trained to the right level, in the right skills, with the right amount of support and supplies to successfully accomplish what the President tasks us to do in the right amount of time…and survive.

Over the past 13 years, the Air Force has performed exceptionally well during combat operations in Iraq and Afghanistan. However, these operations have focused on missions conducted in a permissive air environment and with large footprints for counterinsurgency. This left insufficient time or resources to train across the full range of Air Force missions, especially missions conducted in contested and highly contested environments. To ensure success in future conflicts, we must get back to full-spectrum readiness. We can only get there by funding critical readiness programs such as flying hours, weapon system sustainment, and training ranges, while also balancing deployments and home-station training—in short, reducing operational tempo. This will not be a quick fix; it will take years to recover. If we do not train for scenarios across a range of military operations, including a future high-end fight, we accept unnecessary risk. Risk for the Air Force means we may not get there in time, it may take the joint team longer to win, and our military service members will be placed in greater danger.

FLEET DIVESTMENT

Given the current funding constraints, the Air Force focused on ways to maximize savings while minimizing risk to our joint forces and our ability to support national defense requirements. Every aircraft fleet has substantial fixed costs such as depot maintenance, training programs, software development, weapons integration, spare parts, and logistics support. Large savings are much more feasible to achieve by divesting entire fleets rather than making a partial reduction to a larger fleet. This allows us to achieve savings measured in the billions rather than "just" millions of dollars.

Upon first glance, divesting an entire fleet is undesirable because it removes all of a fleet's capabilities from our range of military options. For example, divesting the A-10 causes a loss of combat-tested aircraft optimized to conduct the close air support mission. However, the A-10 cannot conduct other critical missions, such as air superiority or interdiction, and cannot survive in a highly contested environment. Air superiority, which gives ground and maritime forces freedom from attack and the freedom to attack, is foundational to the way our joint force fights. It cannot be assumed, must be earned and is difficult to maintain. One of the dramatic advantages of airpower in a major campaign is its ability to eliminate second echelon forces and paralyze the enemy's ability to maneuver. As the Air Force becomes smaller, we must retain multi-role aircraft that provide greater flexibility and more options for the joint force commander.

Another example is the Air Force's U-2 and RQ-4 Global Hawk Block 30, high-altitude ISR aircraft. The U-2 has been the combatant commanders' high-altitude ISR platform of choice due to its exceptional reliability, flexibility, survivability, and sensor capabilities. In the current fiscal environment, the Air Force cannot afford to maintain both platforms. While both have performed marvelously in Afghanistan and other theaters worldwide, the Global Hawk RQ-4 Block 30 provides unmatched range and endurance and, after multiple years of focused effort, now comes at a lower cost per flying hour. With responsible investment in sensor enhancements, the Global Hawk RQ-4 Block 30 can meet high-altitude, long endurance ISR requirements. Therefore, long-term affordability after near-term investments provides a stronger case for the RQ-4 Global Hawk Block 30 in a constrained funding environment.

To support combatant commanders and act as good stewards for the taxpayer, we need to divest entire fleets of aircraft to achieve large savings while preserving the capabilities the Air Force uniquely provides to the joint force.

ACTIVE COMPONENT/RESERVE COMPONENT (AC/RC) MIX

American Airmen from each component — Regular Air Force, Air National Guard, and Air Force Reserve — provide seamless airpower on a global scale every day. The uniformed members of today's Total Force consist of approximately 327,600 Regular Air Force Airmen, 105,400 Air National Guardsmen, and 70,400 Air Force Reserve Airmen actively serving in the Selected Reserve, as authorized by the FY14 National Defense Authorization Act (NDAA). Over the past two decades, to meet combatant commander requirements and the demands of recurring deployments, the Air Force has increasingly called upon its Total Force. This elevated use of the Air National Guard and Air Force Reserve has transformed a traditionally strategic reserve force into a force that provides operational capability, strategic depth, and surge capacity. As the Air Force becomes smaller, each component will increase reliance on one another for the success of the overall mission.

To meet Department of Defense (DoD) strategic guidance for a leaner force that remains ready at any size, the Air Force plans to remove approximately 500 aircraft across the inventories of all three components, saving over $9 billion. Additionally, the Air Force has instituted an analytical process of determining the proper mix of personnel and capabilities across the components to meet current and future requirements within available resources. Air Force leadership representing the active and reserve components, including adjutants general, teamed to develop the Air Force FY15 Total Force Proposal (TFP-15) that preserves combat capability and stability for our Total Force. Taking into account recent lessons learned and existing fiscal realities, this compilation of actions maximizes every dollar and leverages opportunities to move personnel and force structure into the reserve component, while still preserving capability and capacity across all three components. To do this, the Air Force plans to transfer aircraft from the active component to the Air National Guard and the Air Force Reserve, including the transfer of flying missions to locations that would otherwise have no mission due to fleet divestments. This effort helps the Air Force maintain combat capability within mandated budgetary constraints by using the strength and unique capabilities of the Guard and Reserve components to make up for capabilities lost as active duty end strength declines, a concept known as compensating leverage. Leaders from all three components developed the TFP-15 plan which accomplishes these objectives using the following principles as guidelines:

- Where possible, replacing divested force structure with like force structure (e.g., A-10 with F-16);
- Adding similar force structure without driving new military construction;
- Adding same-type force structure to units where possible and returning mission sets to locations where they were previously located;

- Considering opportunities to realign force structure to the reserve component prior to any decision to completely divest aircraft; and
- Considering new aircraft deliveries as options for mission transition at uncovered locations.

In January 2013, as part of the Air Force's effort to optimize the capabilities of the active and reserve components, the Secretary of the Air Force (SecAF) and the Chief of Staff of the Air Force (CSAF) established the Total Force Task Force (TF2) to explore and leverage the unique strengths and characteristics of each component. This task force conducted a comprehensive review of Total Force requirements, offered ideas for improving collaboration between the three components, and gave us a starting point for future Total Force analysis and assessment efforts. To continue the body of work initiated by the TF2, and facilitate a transition to a permanent staff structure, the CSAF directed the stand-up of a transitional organization, the Total Force Continuum (TF-C), on October 1, 2013. The TF-C is continuing to develop and refine decision support tools that will help shape and inform the FY16 budget deliberations.

The Air Force has made great strides in understanding how a three-component structure can operate as a powerful, efficient, and cost-effective Service that maximizes the integrated power of our air, space, and cyberspace forces. This needs to be the way we do business, without even thinking about it. We will continue to seek ways to strengthen and institutionalize the collaboration and cooperation between the components, including reviewing the National Commission on the Structure of the Air Force's findings. Our initial examination of the Commission's report suggests a great deal of symmetry between many of their recommendations and current Air Force proposals for the way ahead. The Air Force is committed to ensuring that our Total Force is fully synchronized to deliver an unparalleled array of airpower anywhere in the world.

RECAPITALIZATION VS. MODERNIZATION

One of the most critical judgments in building the Air Force plan for 2015 and beyond was how to balance investment in our current aging fleet against the need to buy equipment that will be viable against future adversaries. Forced to make tough decisions, we favored funding new capabilities (recapitalization) over upgrading legacy equipment (modernization). We cannot afford to bandage old airplanes as potential adversaries roll new ones off the assembly line. For example, the backbone of our bomber and tanker fleets, the B-52 and KC-135, are from the Eisenhower era, and our 4th generation fighters average 25 years of age. That is why our top three acquisition priorities remain the KC-46A aerial tanker, the F-35A Joint Strike Fighter, and the Long Range Strike Bomber (LRS-B).

The KC-46A will begin to replace our aging tanker fleet in 2016, but even when the program is complete in 2028 we will have replaced less than half of the current tanker fleet and will still be flying over 200 KC-135s. Similarly, our average bomber is 32 years old. We need the range, speed, survivability, and punch that the LRS-B will provide. Tankers are the lifeblood of our joint force's ability to respond to crisis and contingencies, and bombers are essential to keeping our Air Force viable as a global force. In our FY15 budget submission, we have fully funded these programs.

The F-35A is also essential to any future conflict with a high-end adversary. The very clear bottom line is that a 4th generation fighter cannot successfully compete with a 5th generation fighter in combat, nor can it survive and operate inside the advanced, integrated air defenses that some countries have today, and many more will have in the future. To defeat those networks, we need the capabilities the F-35A will bring. In response to tightening fiscal constraints, the Air Force has deferred four F-35As in the Future Years Defense Program (FYDP). If the President's projected top-line enhancements are not realized, and future appropriations are set at sequestration-levels, the Air Force may lose up to 19 total F-35As within the FYDP.

Moving forward, we cannot afford to mortgage the future of our Air Force and the defense of our Nation. Recapitalization is not optional— it is required to execute our core missions against a high-end threat for decades to come.

MAKING EVERY DOLLAR COUNT

PROGRAM STEWARDSHIP

The Air Force and our Airmen are committed to being good stewards of every taxpayer dollar. One way we are doing this is by making sound and innovative choices to maximize combat capability within available resources. Recently, the Air Force announced its intent to proceed with the program to ensure the continued availability of the Combat Rescue Helicopter (CRH). The CRH contract award protects a good competitive price and effectively uses the $334 million Congress appropriated to protect the program.

Another example of maximizing the bang out of each taxpayer buck is the KC-46A tanker contract. The recapitalization of the Air Force's tanker fleet is one of our top three priorities, and the fixed-price contract for 179 aircraft represents an outstanding return on investment for the Air Force and the American people. The program is currently on track in cost, schedule, and technical performance, and in the FY15 PB we were able to save $0.9 billion in KC-46A Aircrew Training System and other KC-46A program risk adjustments based on successes to date. Keeping this program on a stable funding path is imperative to meeting our contractual obligations and ultimately to our Air Force's ability to meet national defense requirements.

The Air Force remains committed to delivering space capabilities at a better value to the taxpayer. In cooperation with Congress and the office of the Secretary of Defense, we have used the Efficient Space Procurement strategy to drive down costs of two key satellites, Space-Based Infrared System (SBIRS) and Advanced Extremely High Frequency (AEHF). Through stable research and development funding, block buys, and fiscal authority to smooth our spending profile combined with strong contracting and negotiation approaches using fixed price contracts and "should cost" reviews, the Air Force has been able to achieve significant savings. For satellites 5 and 6 of the AEHF program, these practices reduced Air Force budget requirements $1.6 billion[1] from the original independent cost estimate of the Cost Assessment and Program Evaluation office (CAPE). For SBIRS 5 and 6 these practices have already reduced the budget

---

[1] FY12-FY17 savings

$883 million[2] from the original CAPE estimate and negotiations are still ongoing. Since our policy is to fund to the CAPE independent cost estimates, these savings are real dollars that are now available to reduce the pressure on our budget.

Perhaps the best results are on the Evolved Expendable Launch Vehicle (EELV) program where we have used competition, long term contracts (where there is only one provider), and good understanding of costs to get better deals for the government. This year's budget reduces the program by $1.2 billion. Combined with prior year Air Force reductions and savings for the National Reconnaissance Office, we have reduced the total program by $4.4 billion since its "high water mark" in the FY12 budget. The Air Force remains committed to driving competition into the launch business and we are actively supporting new entrants in their bids for certification. At the same time we must maintain our commitment to mission assurance that has resulted in unprecedented success. We have had 68 successful EELV launches and 30 additional successful National Security Space launches in a row, but we know that the only launch that matters is the next one.

These are just a few examples of how the Air Force is optimizing our allocated resources. Good stewardship of the taxpayer's dollars demands we look for more efficient ways to accomplish the mission as an inherent part of our program and budget decision-making process every year.

ENERGY

To enhance mission capability and readiness, the Air Force is diligently managing our resources including our demand for energy and water. By improving the efficiency of our processes, operations, facilities, and equipment, the Air Force can generate cost savings and decrease our reliance on foreign energy sources. The Air Force has reduced its facility energy consumption by 20 percent since 2003 and has instituted a number of fuel saving initiatives, reducing the amount of fuel our aircraft have consumed by over 647 million gallons since 2006. Additionally, we are investing $1.4 billion across the FYDP for next generation jet engine technology that promises reduced fuel consumption, lower maintenance costs, and helps ensure a robust industrial base. By instituting aircraft and installation efficiencies over the past five years, we avoided an energy bill $2.2 billion higher in 2013 than it would have been otherwise.

BASE REALIGNMENT AND CLOSURE (BRAC)

As we make efforts to become more efficient by improving and sustaining our installations, we also recognize we carry infrastructure that is excess to our needs. The Air Force is fully involved in the office of the Secretary of Defense led European Infrastructure Consolidation efforts. Since 1990, the Air Force has decreased European main operating bases from 25 to 6, returning more than 480 sites to their respective host nations and reduced Air Force personnel in Europe by almost 70 percent. While we have made large reductions in base infrastructure overseas, and previous BRAC rounds made some progress in reducing U.S. infrastructure, we still spend more than $7 billion operating, sustaining, recapitalizing, and modernizing our physical plants across the Air Force each year. While our best efforts to use innovative programs have paid dividends,

---

[2] FY13-FY18 savings

such as recapitalizing our housing through privatization and pursuing public-public and public-private partnerships, we continue to spend money maintaining excess infrastructure that would be better spent recapitalizing and sustaining weapons systems, training for readiness, and investing in our Airmen's quality of life needs. The Air Force has limited authority under current public law to effectively consolidate military units or functions and then divest real property when no longer needed. To save considerable resources, we request BRAC authority in 2017.

MILITARY COMPENSATION

Military compensation has risen over the last decade and has helped the Air Force to recruit and retain a world class force in the midst of an extended period of high operations tempo. To sustain the recruitment and retention of Airmen committed to serve the Nation, military compensation must remain highly competitive. However, in light of projected constraints on future defense spending, DoD needs to slow the rate of growth in military compensation in order to avoid deeper reductions to force structure, readiness, and modernization efforts critical to support the warfighter and the national defense. The Air Force supports the military compensation recommendations and will reinvest the savings back into readiness to provide our Airmen with the necessary resources to remain the best equipped and best trained Air Force in the world.

AIRMEN

INNOVATIVE FORCE

We are the best Air Force in the world because of our Airmen. We continue to attract, recruit, develop, and train Airmen with strong character who are honor bound, on and off-duty, by the Air Force's core values of *Integrity First, Service Before Self,* and *Excellence in All We Do.* We depend on a workforce that leads cutting-edge research, explores emerging technology areas, and promotes innovation across government, industry, and academia.

The budgetary constraints in FY14 and beyond force the Air Force to become smaller. However, as we shrink, we must continue to recruit and retain men and women with the right balance of skills to meet Air Force mission requirements, and maintain a ready force across the full-spectrum of operations. Attracting science, technology, engineering, and mathematics (STEM) talent to our civilian workforce has been hampered by furloughs, hiring and pay freezes, and lack of professional development opportunities. Despite fiscal constraints, the Air Force needs to continue to attract and nurture our Nation's best and brightest into both our military and our civilian workforces, because it is our innovative Airmen who continue to make our Air Force the best in the world.

AIRMEN AND FAMILY SUPPORT

Airmen and their families are our most important resource. We are committed to fostering a culture of dignity and respect, and to ensuring an environment where all Airmen have the opportunity to excel. As a result, the Air Force will preserve our core services programs (fitness, childcare, and food services) and warfighter and family support programs. Unfortunately, the budget environment necessitates consequential reductions to morale, welfare, and recreation programs at U.S.-based installations to affect cost savings. We will do so in a manner that provides commanders as much flexibility as possible to respond to their individual military community needs and unique geographic situations.

AIR FORCE SEXUAL ASSAULT PREVENTION AND RESPONSE

The Air Force's mission depends on Airmen having complete trust and confidence in one another. Our core values of *Integrity, Service* and *Excellence,* define the standard. Sexual assault is absolutely inconsistent and incompatible with our core values, our mission, and our heritage. As such, our SAPR program is a priority both for ensuring readiness and taking care of our Airmen.

During the last year, the Air Force has worked hard to combat sexual assault. We have invested in programmatic, educational, and resourcing efforts aimed at reinforcing a zero tolerance environment. Our SAPR office now reports directly to the Vice Chief of Staff of the Air Force. We revamped our wing and group commanders' and senior non-commissioned officers' sexual assault response training courses, established full-time victim advocates with comprehensive training and accreditation requirements, and implemented the Defense Sexual Assault Incident Database to streamline data collection and reporting efforts.

The Air Force has been DoD's leader in special victim capabilities, particularly with the success of the Air Force's Special Victim's Counsel (SVC) program. The SVC program provides victims with a dedicated legal advocate whose sole job is to help the victim through the often traumatizing legal process following an assault. So far the results have been exceptional. Since the program's implementation, more than 565 Airmen have benefited from SVC services, and in FY13, 92 percent of the victims reported that they were "extremely satisfied" with SVC support. Due to its success, the Secretary of Defense has directed all Services to stand up similar SVC programs. The Air Force has also established a team of 10 Special Victims' Unit senior trial counsels and 24 Air Force Office of Special Investigations agents who have received advanced education and training to work sexual assault cases.

Providing a safe, respectful, and productive work environment free from sexual innuendo, harassment, and assault is the responsibility of every Airman, and the Air Force is committed to realizing this vision.

DIVERSITY

The Nation's demographics are rapidly changing, and the makeup of our Air Force must reflect and relate to the population it serves. To leverage the strengths of diversity throughout our Air Force, our leaders must develop and retain talented individuals with diverse backgrounds and experiences, and create inclusive environments where all Airmen feel valued and able to contribute to the mission. Air Force decision-making and operational capabilities are enhanced by enabling varied perspectives and potentially creative solutions to complex problems. Moreover, diversity is critical for successful international operations, as cross-culturally competent Airmen build partnerships and conduct the full range of military operations globally.

The competition for exceptional diverse talent will remain fierce. To compete with other government agencies and the business sector to attract and recruit the Nation's finest talent, the Air Force must develop an accessions strategy that taps new markets of diverse, high performing youth. In a similar sense, the Air Force must continue targeted development of existing talent, and continue to promote a comprehensive mentorship program that trains all Airmen to view operational problems and opportunities through a diversity lens.

FORCE MANAGEMENT

In FY14 and FY15, we will implement a number of force management programs designed to reduce the overall size of the force while maintaining our combat capability. The goal of these programs is to make reductions through voluntary separations and retirements, maximizing voluntary incentives to ensure a smooth transition for our Airmen. To meet current funding constraints, significant reductions in total end strength over the FYDP are required, and may impact up to 25,000 Airmen. These reductions are driven largely by the divestiture of associated force structure and weapons systems, headquarters realignment, and a rebalancing of aircrew-to-cockpit ratios in a post-Afghanistan environment. Realignment efforts will also reduce Headquarters Air Force funding by 20 percent immediately and combatant command headquarters funding through a 4 percent annual reduction reaching 20 percent by FY19. We have developed a plan to retain high performing Airmen so that we can accomplish the mission our Nation expects.

AMERICA'S AIR FORCE

A GLOBAL, READY FORCE

Over the past 35 years, the Air Force has been called upon more than 150 times to conduct combat or humanitarian operations in more than 50 countries around the world. It is impossible to predict when America will call on its Air Force next. It is our job to be ready.

The evolving complexity and potentially quick onset of warfare means that future conflicts will be a "come as you are" fight. There will be precious little time to "spin up" units that are unready to carry out their designated missions. Currently, the combatant commanders' requirement for fighter squadrons essentially equals the number of squadrons in the Air Force, and the requirement for bomber aircraft and ISR platforms is much greater than the number currently in the inventory. In simple economic terms, our supply across Air Force capabilities is less than or equal to the demand. Tiered readiness is not an option; your Air Force is either ready or it is not.

AIR FORCE CORE MISSIONS

Airmen bring five interdependent and integrated core missions to the Nation's military portfolio. These core missions have endured since President Truman originally assigned airpower roles and missions to the Air Force in 1947. While our sister Services operate efficiently within the air, space, and cyber domains, the Air Force is the only Service that provides an integrated capability on a worldwide scale. Although the way we operate will constantly evolve, the Air Force will continue to perform these missions so that our military can respond quickly and appropriately to unpredictable threats and challenges.

Air and Space Superiority…Freedom from Attack and the Freedom to Attack

Air and space superiority has long provided our Nation an asymmetric advantage. The Air Force's FY15 budget request focuses on the capabilities necessary to ensure we can provide the theater-wide air and space superiority our combatant commanders require.

Since April 1953, roughly seven million American service members have deployed to combat and contingency operations all over the world. Thousands of them have died in combat. Not a single one was killed by bombs from an enemy aircraft. Air superiority is a fundamental pillar of airpower and a prerequisite to the American way of modern, joint warfare—we cannot fail. In calendar year 2013 (CY13), the Air Force flew over 27,000 air superiority sorties, accounting for over 37,000 flight hours. These sorties directly supported critical missions, such as homeland air sovereignty with Operation NOBLE EAGLE and the protection of the President of the United States. Additionally, the Air Force flew numerous Theater Security Posture missions in the Central Command and Pacific Command areas of responsibility.

To ensure we can provide unmatched air superiority capability and manage the risk associated with combat force reductions and emerging advanced technologies, the Air Force is modernizing munitions and platforms. In FY15, the Air Force continues to invest in the AIM-120D and AIM-9X air-to-air missiles and develop new munitions to address future threats. Upgrades to the F-22 program and the procurement of the F-35A will also provide required capabilities to help ensure freedom of movement in contested environments. Continued upgrades to 4th generation platforms, such as the Joint Air-to-Surface Standoff Missile Extended Range for the F-16, are also necessary to ensure sustained viability in the future. These added capabilities will ensure the Air Force is prepared to survive today and meet tomorrow's challenges for control of the air.

America's freedom to operate effectively across the spectrum of conflict also includes its ability to exploit space. Every day joint, interagency, and coalition forces depend on Air Force space operations to perform their missions on every continent, in the air, on the land, and at sea. In CY13, the Air Force launched 8 National Security Space (NSS) missions totaling 68 consecutive successful Evolved Expendable Launch Vehicle launches to date and 98 consecutive successful NSS missions. In FY15, the Air Force will acquire three launch services and plans to launch 10 NSS missions. The Air Force will also continue the evaluation and certification of potential new entrants.

The space environment is more congested, contested, and competitive than ever, requiring the Air Force to focus on Space Situational Awareness (SSA). Our SSA modernization efforts include: moving forward with acquisition of the Space Fence (near-Earth SSA capability); defining the Space-Based Space Surveillance follow-on system; fielding the Geosynchronous Space Situational Awareness Program; continuing work with our Australian partners to field an advanced space surveillance telescope (deep-space SSA capabilities); and fielding the Joint Space Operations Center mission system (SSA command and control and data integration and exploitation).

The Air Force remains fully committed to the long-term goal of fostering international relationships and supporting ongoing security efforts with partner nations around the globe. Teaming with allies and partners not only helps cost and risk-sharing, it also increases capability and capacity to support contingency operations. Space is an area in which we have made significant progress in building partnerships.

Underpinning all of these capabilities is our ability to effectively operate in and through cyberspace. The advantages of effective cyberspace operations in speed, ubiquity, access, stealth, surprise, real-time battlespace awareness and information exchange, and command and control are manifest in every Air Force mission area and nearly every mission area has come to depend on them. Global strike; fused intelligence, surveillance, and reconnaissance; force and personnel movement; telemedicine; global logistics; financial systems; joint aerial network linkages; space control; remotely piloted aircraft and vehicle command and control; target deconfliction; fires coordination; and even aspects of national strategic (including nuclear) command and control, rely on cyberspace superiority. Despite the strategic risk this dependence introduces, the advantages to those mission areas are too great to forego, so the Air Force must continue to lead and leverage the advantages of cyberspace superiority.

Intelligence, Surveillance, and Reconnaissance...Delivering Decision Advantage

Air Force globally integrated ISR provides commanders at every level with the knowledge they need to prevent strategic surprise, make decisions, command forces, and employ weapons. Our ISR Airmen identify and assess adversary targets and vulnerabilities from hideouts to bunkers to mobile launchers with greater accuracy than ever seen in the history of warfare. In 2013 alone, Airmen flew over 27,000 ISR missions, enabled the removal of 1,500 enemy combatants from the fight, provided critical adversary awareness and targeting intelligence to U.S. and coalition forces in over 350 troops-in-contact engagements, enhanced battlespace awareness through 630,000 hours of sustained overwatch of tactical forces and communication lines, and identified over 350 weapons caches and explosive devices that would have otherwise targeted American and partner forces. ISR reduces uncertainty about our adversaries and their capabilities, strengthens deterrence, prompts adversaries to act more cautiously, provides intelligence that allows commanders a decision-making advantage, and delivers real-time information on which troops rely to fight effectively and win.

In recent years, the development of Air Force ISR capabilities has focused mainly on meeting the needs of permissive combat environments. In more contested future environments, gaining and maintaining an ISR advantage will become increasingly difficult and even more important. Therefore, the Air Force will focus primarily on enhancing ISR capabilities for operations in contested environments. Accomplishing this will require updating the current mix of ISR assets, while also giving significant and sustained attention to modernizing Air Force ISR systems, capabilities, and analytical capacity.

Rapid Global Mobility...Delivery on Demand

The Air Force's rapid global mobility capability is truly unique. There is no other force in the world that would have the confidence to place its fighting men and women at the end of an 8,000 mile logistical train. The fact that we are able to reliably supply a military force of 100,000[3] troops in a landlocked country half a world away during an active fight is simply amazing.

On any given day, Airmen deliver critical personnel and cargo and provide airdrop of time-sensitive supplies, food, and ammunition on a global scale. Averaging one take-off or landing every two minutes, every day of the year, America's mobility fleet provides a capability unmatched by any air force across the globe. Whether it is sustaining the warfighter in any environment or delivering hope with humanitarian assistance, our Airmen ensure that the whole of government and international partners are strengthened with this unique capability to get assets to the fight quickly, remain in the fight, and return home safely.

In CY13, Airmen flew 26,000 airlift missions, and over the course of 345 airdrops, the Air Force dropped 11 million pounds of combat-enabling sustainment to coalition forces on the ground in Afghanistan. As the linchpin to power projection at intercontinental distances, Air Force tanker crews flew 31,700 missions and aeromedical evacuation crews airlifted 5,163 wounded Soldiers, Sailors, Airmen, Marines, and injured civilians around the globe. Since 9/11, America's tanker fleet has offloaded over 2.69 billion gallons of fuel to joint and coalition air forces, and the Air Force has logged an astounding 194,300 patient movements.

To ensure global reach, the Air Force will continue to protect this vital mission by recapitalizing our aging aerial tanker fleet with the KC-46A, modernizing the inter-theater airlift fleet, and continue supporting the C-130J multi-year procurement contract that will extend beyond FY18.

Global Strike...Any Target, Any Time

The Air Force's nuclear and conventional precision strike forces can credibly threaten and effectively hold any target on the planet at risk and, if necessary, disable or destroy it promptly— even from bases in the continental United States. These forces possess the unique ability to achieve tactical, operational, and strategic effects all in the course of a single combat mission. Whether employed from forward bases or enabled by in-flight refueling, global strike missions include a wide range of crisis response and escalation control options, such as providing close air support to troops at risk, interdicting enemy forces, supporting special operations forces, and targeting an adversary's vital centers. These capabilities, unmatched by any other nation's air force, will be of growing importance as America rebalances its force structure and faces potential adversaries that are modernizing their militaries to deny access to our forces.

In CY13, the Air Force flew 21,785 close air support sorties in Operation ENDURING FREEDOM, including over 1,400 sorties with at least one weapons release. In the rebalance to the Pacific, the Air Force rotated five fighter squadrons and three bomber squadrons to forward

---

[3] At their peak, U.S. military forces in Afghanistan consisted of 100,000 military members and over 112,000 contractors. Source: CRS 2011 report "DoD Contractors in Afghanistan and Iraq"

locations in Guam, Japan, and Korea to project power and reassure our regional partners and flew over 43,000 missions bolstering theater security and stability. We continue to invest in the Pacific theater to ensure viability of our Air Force bases through a combination of hardening, dispersal, and active defenses.

The Air Force will focus future efforts on modernizing global strike assets to ensure that American forces are prepared to act when, where, and how they are needed. The multi-role F-35A is the centerpiece of the Air Force's future precision attack capability, designed to penetrate air defenses and deliver a wide range of precision munitions. Procuring the F-35A aircraft remains a top priority, and we plan to achieve initial operational capability in 2016.

The backbone of America's nuclear deterrence is the ICBM fleet. To ensure the ICBM's viability through 2030, the Air Force will invest in updated warhead fuzes, as well as beginning guidance and propulsion modernization programs and modernization of launch facilities and communication centers. While the LRS-B is the bomber of the future, the Air Force will continue to modernize current B-2 and B-52 aircraft to keep these nuclear capabilities viable. The Air Force will ensure we are able to maintain the flexibility to deploy nuclear forces in a manner that best serves our national security interests.

Command and Control...Total Flexibility

Air Force command and control systems provide commanders the ability to conduct highly coordinated joint operations on an unequaled scale. Getting the right information to the right person at the right time is essential to the American way of war. The capability to deliver airpower is also intimately dependent on the ability to operate effectively in cyberspace, a domain in and through which we conduct all of our core missions and which is critical to our command and control. Operations in cyberspace magnify military effects by increasing the efficiency and effectiveness of air and space operations and by integrating capabilities across all domains. However, the Nation's advantage in command and control is under constant attack with new and more capable threats emerging daily in the areas of cyber weapons, anti-satellite systems, and electromagnetic jamming. Our adversaries are making advances by electronically linking their own combat capabilities, which create new military challenges.

To counter these challenges, the Air Force will prioritize development and fielding of advanced command and control systems that are highly capable, reliable, resilient, and interoperable, while retaining the minimum command and control capacity to meet national defense requirements. More importantly, we will recruit and train innovative Airmen with the expertise to build, manage, secure, and advance our complex and diverse command and control systems.

CONCLUSION

Ultimately, our job is to fight and win the Nation's wars. While, the Air Force's FY15 budget submission remains strategy-based, it is also shaped by the fiscal environment. At the levels requested in the President's budget, the Air Force protects the capabilities required to prevail in the more demanding operational environment in years to come. By making tough choices today we set ourselves on a path to produce a ready and modernized Air Force that is smaller, yet still lethal against potential adversaries in the future. Regardless of the strategic tradeoffs made, at sequestration-levels it is not possible to budget for an Air Force that is capable of simultaneously performing all of the missions our Nation expects. We would end up with a force that is less ready, less capable, less viable and unable to fully execute the defense strategy. While we would still have the world's finest Air Force able to deter adversaries, we would also expect to suffer greater losses in scenarios against more modern threats.

Airpower…because without it, you lose!